TECHNOLOGY
in today's
MUSIC
CLASSROOM

Active Music Making
with Tablets, Projectors, Computers,
and Interactive Whiteboards

BY MANJU DURAIRAJ

HAL•LEONARD®
CORPORATION

ISBN-13: 978-1-48039-142-0

Published by Hal Leonard Corporation
7777 W. Bluemound Road
P.O. Box 13819
Milwaukee, WI 53213

Library of Congress Cataloging-in-Publication Data

Durairaj, Manju.
  Technology in today's music classroom : active music making with tablets, projectors, computers and interactive whiteboards / By Manju Durairaj. -- First edition.
    pages cm
  Includes bibliographical references.
  ISBN 978-1-4803-9142-0
1. Music--Instruction and study--Technological innovations. 2. Interactive whiteboards. I. Title.
MT1.D865 2014
780.71--dc23
                                2014033456

Printed in the U.S.A.
First Edition

HAL•LEONARD®
Visit Hal Leonard Online at **www.halleonard.com**

In Australia Contact:

Hal Leonard Australia Pty. Ltd.
4 Lentara Court
Cheltenham, Victoria, 3192 Australia
Email: ausadmin@halleonard.com.au

TABLE OF CONTENTS

INTRODUCTION

Technology is just one tool that is used by 21st century educators and students. It can be a powerful aid to facilitate learning and teaching without compromising active music making – the core of general music education. Utilizing technology optimally is a skill that can be easily acquired. General music students can create, sing, move, dance, play instruments, notate and listen, even as the teacher uses technology-based medium to optimize and enrich student learning.

This book aims to provide educators with basic tools to create powerful visual lesson presentations for engaging every type of learner. Each chapter deals with creating lessons using available technology and applications.

EDITOR'S NOTE: This teacher resource specifically references Microsoft Word, PowerPoint and SMART Notebook software. Many of the tips and techniques presented here are also available in other text, presentation and interactive software applications. Use the inspirations presented here to experiment in other software and add new features to your own creations.

ABOUT THE WRITER

Manju Durairaj was born and raised in India. She studied in Pune, India. She was involved in graduate research projects on comparative pedagogical practices of Indian (Carnatic) and Western Music at Middlesex University, London, UK. She graduated with her second master's degree and K-12 certification from VanderCook College of Music, Chicago. Manju is also certified in Orff-Schulwerk, completing her levels at George Mason University, with master classes at University of St. Thomas, and at the Orff Institute in Salzburg, Austria.

Manju currently teaches Pre K-5 general music at the Latin School of Chicago. She is past president of the Greater Chicago Orff Chapter. She is a SMART certified trainer and customizes these training courses for music educators. She teaches technology (IWB/tablets), movement, and general music summer and weekend teacher training courses at VanderCook College of Music, Chicago. She has presented at ISME, AOSA, OAKE, NAfME, MKMEA, IMEA, ILMEA, WMEA, and other state conferences. She has been published in the *Orff Echo, Reverberations*, and the *Bulletin of the Council for Research in Music Education*.

CHAPTER 1
Projector and Computer

HARDWARE
- LCD projector
- Laptop/desktop computer
- Sound source (through computer/laptop, or boom box, or smartphone/tablet connected to speakers)

SOFTWARE
- Microsoft Word
- Microsoft PowerPoint

ROOM SET-UP
Teacher has access to an LCD projector connected to a computer/laptop.

PRIOR KNOWLEDGE OF WORD
- Opening a new file
- Copy and Paste functions

PRIOR KNOWLEDGE OF POWERPOINT
- Opening a new presentation
- Inserting new slides
- Copy and Paste functions
- Playing Slide Show

IN THIS CHAPTER
- Create Shapes in Word
- Activities Using Shapes
  - Move and Freeze
  - Instrument Play and Stop
  - Extensions
- Create Rhythm Flashcards
- Create Shapes and Animations in PowerPoint

- Activities Using Animations
  - Rhythm Pulse
  - Create a Xylophone Animation
  - Improvisation With Xylophone Visual
  - Create a Vocal Exploration Using Animated Pathways

CREATE SHAPES IN WORD

- Create a new Word document.

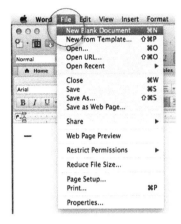

- Select the Home button from the top menu bar.

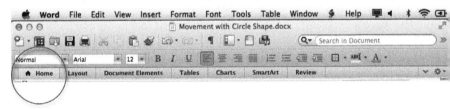

- Select the Shapes tool from the contextual toolbar that is the extended menu that drops down when the Home button is selected.

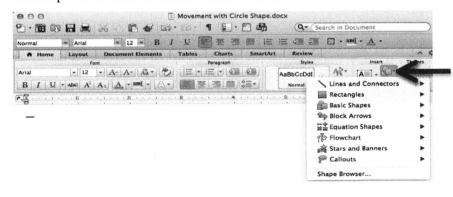

- Select the Oval from the Basic Shapes submenu.

- Insert the oval shape into the document and extend it until it makes a circle.

- Select the object and the Format button appears next to the Home button or Right-click or Control-click the object and select the Format Shape button.

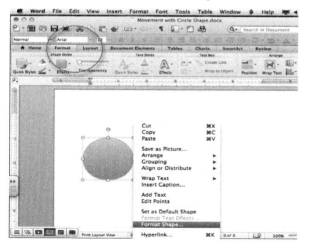

7

- Select the Paint Bucket to access the color palette.

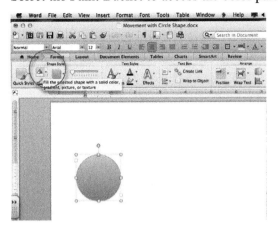

- Click on a color of choice.

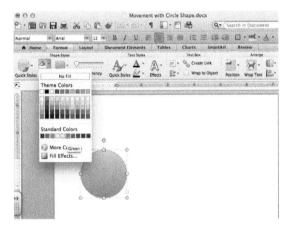

- Choose a color for the shape.

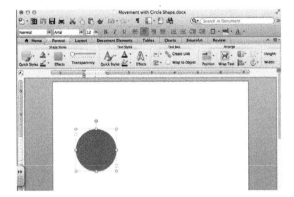

- Select, Copy and Paste the circle.

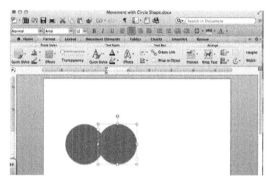

- Format the second shape, filling it with a different color and space it away from the first.

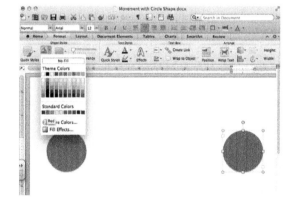

- Add text beneath the shapes.

ACTIVITIES USING SHAPES

Move and Freeze

- Brainstorm possible movement words with the class, print and place them in a place visible to students.

Locomotor (traveling)

Walk (backwards, sideways)

Gallop	Leap
Crawl	skip

Non-Locomotor (in place)

Shake	Wave
Shimmy	Jog
Jump	Hop

- Select a piece of music, and play the Freeze Game.
- Pre-determine whether it will be a locomotor or non-locomotor movement game.
- Point or touch the Green Shape for a few phrases, and students can move. When the Red Shape is touched, students freeze.

Instrument Play and Stop

- Use the same Red and Green Shape visual.
- Distribute un-pitched percussion instruments like hand drums, to the entire class if enough instruments are available, or to a small group if a limited number of instruments are available.
- Let students explore and brainstorm how to play the drums, tap the edge on the floor, swish their hands across the surface, tap with the fingertips etc.
- Display these choices where they will be visible.
- Choose a student to be the conductor.
- When student conductor points to the Green Shape, the class plays the drums. When conductor points to the Red Shape, the class stops playing.
- Play this game without a set pattern or rhythm.

Extension of Instrument Play and Stop

- Let the conductor decide the dynamic (loud or soft) or tempo (fast, medium or slow), and play the game.
- Let the conductor or another student decide how to play the drum. For example, just using the fingertips, striking the center or the edge, rubbing the palm of the hand on the surface of the drum.
- After multiple students have had a chance to be the conductor, extend the activity to include rhythm.

Further Extension

- Review 4-beat rhythm patterns that students know, speak a rhythm pattern, or print out and display patterns that students know. For example:

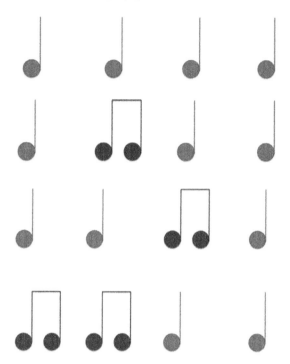

- Choose a pattern or let the student conductor pick the pattern. Play the Freeze Game again with un-pitched instruments.
- To create flashcards like the ones in the example above, see the Create Rhythm Flashcards section on the next page.

CREATE RHYTHM FLASHCARDS

- Create a Circle Shape and fill it with a color of choice. From the Shapes submenu, select the Line Shape and draw it over the circle.

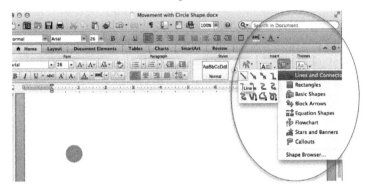

- Select the line and format the color.

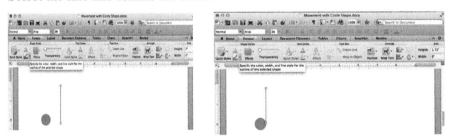

- Select both the circle and the line by holding down the Shift Key while clicking first on one object then the other.

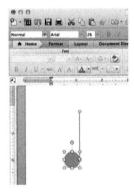

- Right-click or Control-click the objects to reveal the dropdown menu.

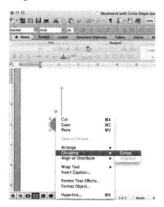

- Select the Grouping option, and group the circle and line to form a note.

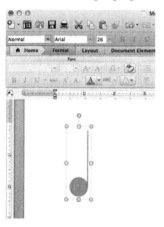

- Copy and Paste two more notes, draw a line across the top of their stems.

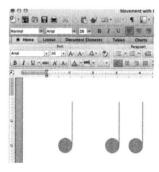 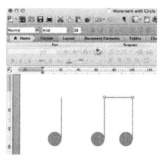

- Format the line color, select both notes and the beam, by shift-clicking on all three, and group them together.

- A 2-beat flashcard has now been created.
- Copy and Paste the quarter and eighth notes to create 2, 3, or 4-beat flashcards with various combinations of quarter and eighth notes.

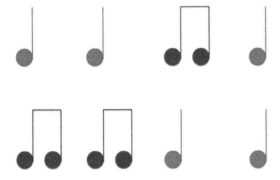

CREATE SHAPES AND ANIMATIONS IN POWERPOINT

Many of the tools and functions in Word, may be transferred to PowerPoint. However, PowerPoint has powerful animation capabilities in addition to many other presentation features.

This section illustrates creating shapes or inserting clipart, and animating these objects for vocal exploration activities. These may be used for tracking high and low pitches on a 2-line staff, and finally transferring them as the solfege pitches so-mi, that may be played on a xylophone. Xylophone playing on the correct bars may be reinforced using animations where bars that should be played change color, or if the xylophone is to be set up in a pentatonic pattern, the unwanted bars may fly off the screen.

Rhythm - Pulse Animation

- Create a new presentation.

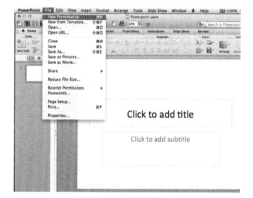

- Select the title and subtitle boxes, and delete them to clear a work area.

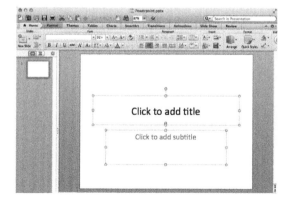

- Click the Home button to view the Shapes option. Select Heart from the Basic Shapes submenu.

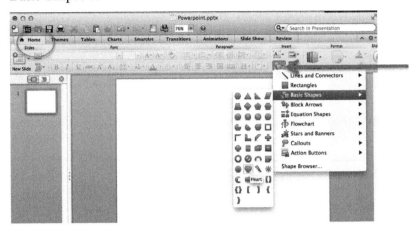

- Draw a heart and select it by clicking on it.

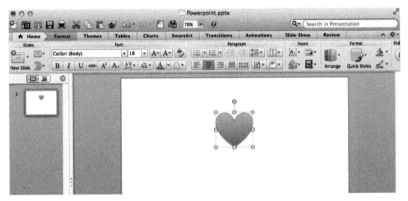

- Format the heart by selecting the Format button, and selecting the Fill option.

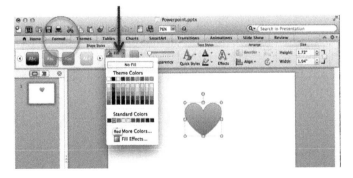

- Further format it by selecting the Line option, and choosing a dark outline.

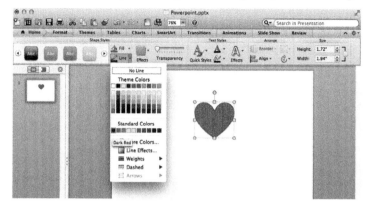

- To Animate the Heart, go to the Animations button on the top menu bar.

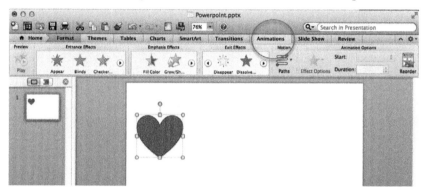

- Select the Heart, select Appear from the Entrance Effects option.

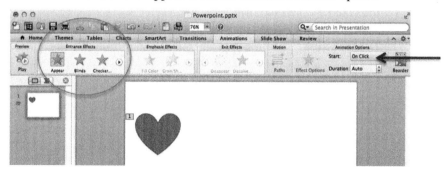

- Note that a colored box with the number 1 appears. This is the first animation to happen on the screen. Also note, in presentation mode, the animation will Start On Click, that is, by touching the space bar or by clicking if using a remote.

- Copy and Paste the Heart. Note that the second Heart has 2 by it, indicating it is the second animation to appear.

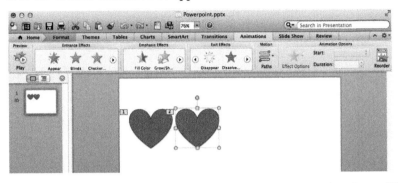

- Copy and Paste two more hearts and space them. Note that they will appear in their numerical order on Click.

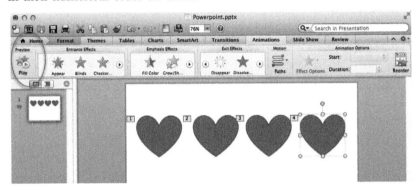

- The animations may be Previewed at any time using the Preview/ Play option indicated by the blue oval.
- Go to Slide Show mode and Click on the Space Bar to view each heart that appear in succession. The timing of the pulse is controlled by presenter clicks.

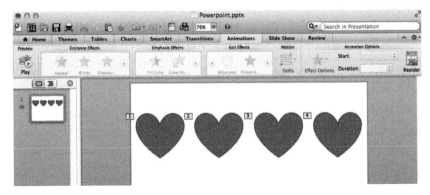

ACTIVITIES USING ANIMATIONS

Rhythm Pulse

- Create 16 of the animated Hearts, and have students say 'doop' when each appears.
- Students can track each heart/pulse. This activity facilitates tracking/ reading from left to right for younger children. Make the first heart of each line a little darker to emphasize the downbeat.

Extension: One Heart at a Time

If it is too visually stimulating to have all the pulses/hearts appear on the screen, the animations can be modified so that only one heart appears at a time on clicking.

- Create a Heart, select it by clicking on it, then Copy and Paste it.

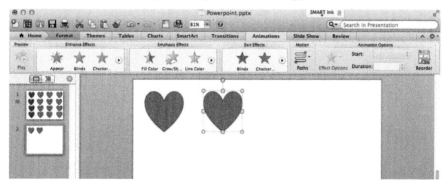

- Animate the first heart to Appear (Entrance Effects), then Disappear (Exit Effects). Note that the Disappear is animation number 2.

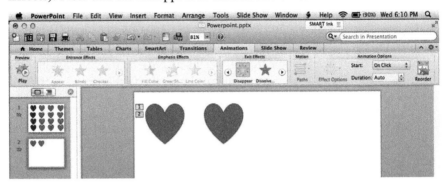

- Select the second Heart and animate it to Appear, but under Animations Options, select the With Previous option. This ensures that the second heart will appear simultaneously as the first disappears.

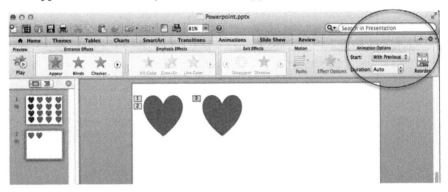

- Select the second Heart again, and animate it to disappear On Click. This is animation Number 3.

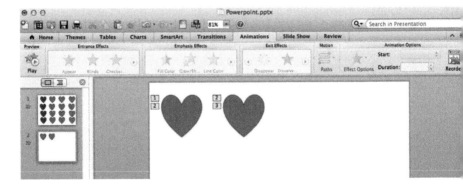

- Select Click, Copy and Paste the second Heart a couple of times. The animations will automatically reorder themselves.

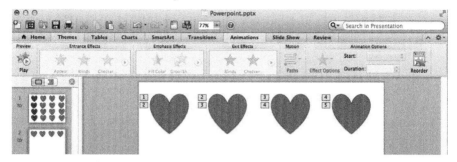

- Copy and Paste as many of these as needed.

Create a Xylophone Animation

A xylophone visual facilitates playing enormously. If a piece is in a pentatonic scale and xylophones need to have certain bars removed, or only certain bars need to be played as an accompaniment, then an animation can be a tremendous visual aid.

- Create a rectangle using the Shapes browser.

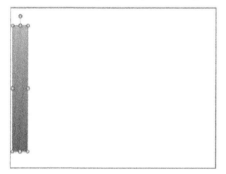

- Copy and Paste this, so that there are 13 rectangles.

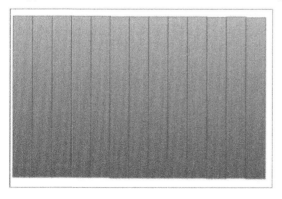

- Select all the rectangles and fill them with a color of choice.

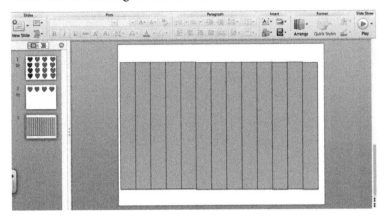

- Select each rectangle and using the handles, arrange them in a descending order or height. Ensure that the width stays the same.

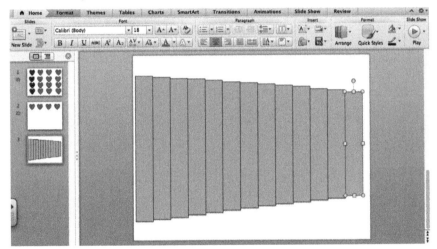

- Create text boxes with the letters C, D, E and so on.

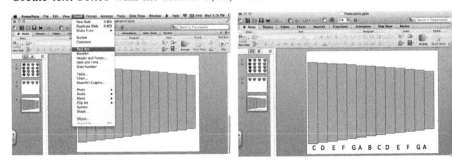

• Move the letters over the bars and position them where needed.

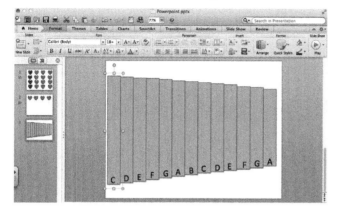

• Select each bar and its text letter, by holding down Shift while clicking on the objects, Right-click and Group them.

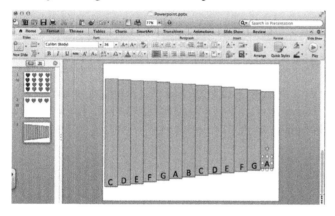

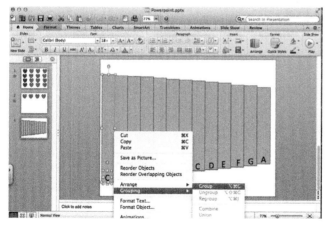

- If the visual is to set up the xylophone in C pentatonic scale, with the F and B bars removed, select the F and B bars by pressing Shift and Clicking on all three bars.

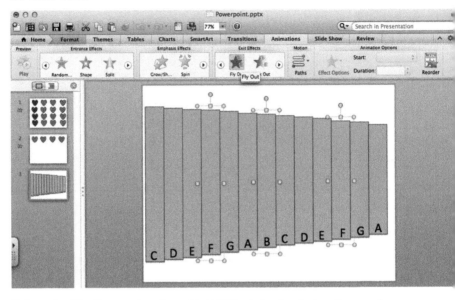

- Select the Fly Out option from Exit Effects in the Animations submenu. Once the Number 1 appears on the selected bars, go to the Effect Options menu and select the direction the bars need to Fly Out.

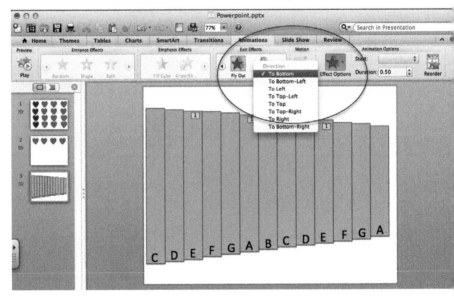

- When the animation is applied the visual will look like this.

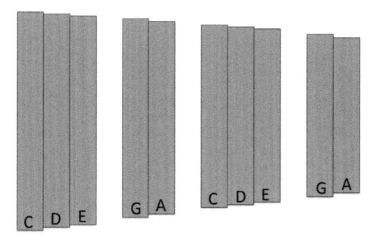

Improvisation with Xylophone Visual

Tinker, Tailor,
Soldier, Sailor,
Rich man, Poor man
Beggarman, Thief

- Students pat the beat and say the poem.
- Students walk the beat and say the poem.
- Students pat the beat and clap the rhythm of the poem.
- Students walk the beat and clap the rhythm of the poem.
- Students identify the eighth beats and quarter rest in the last line.
- Once rhythm is secure, send the students to the instruments.
- Ask them to 'helicopter' off the B,F,F bars. Helicopter: place one hand on each end of the bar and lift it up off the instrument.
- Review mallet technique with younger students and "airplay" the rhythm.
- Demonstrate the rhythm on the xylophone on first the so-la (G, A) bars.
- Ask students to play the rhythm on the two bars.
- Demonstrate the rhythm on the mi-re-do bars (C,D,E).
- Ask the students to explore the rhythm using just the three bars
- Then expand the scale, and ask them to explore the rhythm on an adjacent set of 3 and 2 bars, do-re-mi so-la (CDE GA) which is the pentatonic scale with do = C.
- Ask students to create a melody with the rhythm, and try to remember it.
- Ask students to then modify their melody to end on do or C.
- Ask students to try to begin and end on do or C.
- Ask for volunteers to share their melody.
- A good melody is one others can remember and perhaps play back.

Create a Vocal Exploration Using Animated Pathways

- Choose a 24-pointed star from the Shapes browser.

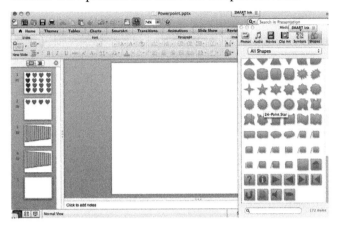

- Insert it into the clear slide, and Format it to create a Fuzz ball. Fill in the shape with Green and outline with Yellow.

• From the Animations Bar, choose the Motion Paths option.

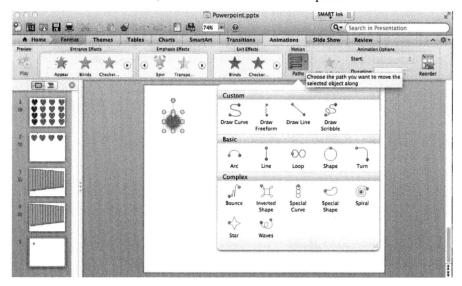

• If the Fuzz ball is to first go down then up, select the Draw Line option.

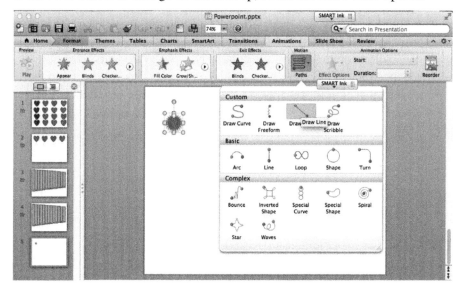

- Once the Draw Line option is selected, the cursor becomes a cross hair. Click on the Fuzz ball and draw a straight line down.

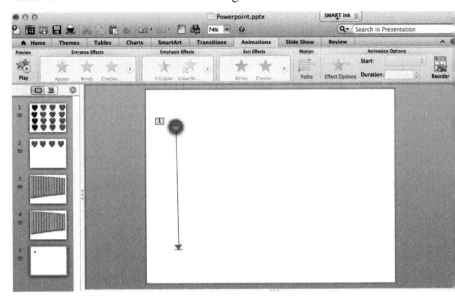

- A Number 1 appears along with a dotted line arrow, with a green starting point and a red ending point.
- A vocal exploration pathway needs to be slow so students have time to vocalize. Select the Number 1 animation box so it is yellow, go to the Durations button in Animation Options and increase the time to 3 or 4.

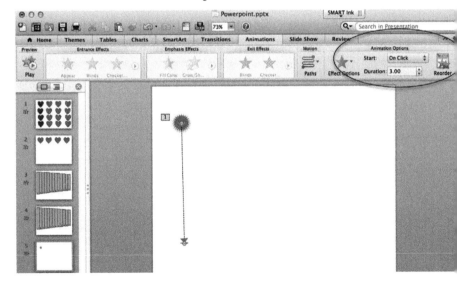

- The same steps may be used to make the Fuzz ball travel up. However position the Fuzz ball at the bottom of the page before animating it.
- The Motion Paths options include Free Scribble, which allows a path to be drawn.
- A horizontal line from left to right provides good practice in sustaining a vocable on a single pitch.

VOCAL EXPLORATION ACTIVITY

- Prepare 5 or more slides with the Fuzz ball moving around a different pathway on each slide.
- Have students sit up nice and tall. Create a story for the Fuzz Ball. Perhaps he is from the Planet of Fuzz and is bouncing around looking for a way to go home; or he's so happy to see the students that he is going to do a happy dance each time they spot him.
- Solicit responses for the initial position of the Fuzz ball, and ask for predictions on which way he will travel – up, or down, or in a straight horizontal line sideways. This prepares students to acquire basic pitch vocabulary – going up, going down and staying the same.
- Choose a vocable like "Wheee" or "Oooooo". Ask students to point to the Fuzz ball. Prepare a starting pitch, and have the students vocally track the Fuzz ball.
- Repeat the process for other slides.

CHAPTER 2
Projector and Tablet

This chapter will illustrate how to create activities, templates, and digital manipulatives, and how to transfer these onto tablets. A whiteboard app on the tablets may be used to teach, reinforce, assess, record audio/video and create screencasts that may be saved onto individual digital portfolios.

HARDWARE
- LCD Projector
- Tablet
- Computer
- VGA cable to connect tablet to projector (optional)

APPS
- Reflector – to project one to four tablets on the screen
  - Note: This app may be used in conjunction with a computer. All devices need to be on the same wireless network.
- Dropbox (optional)
- Email (optional)
- Google Drive (optional)
- Photo Browser – available on tablet
- Whiteboard apps referenced
  - iPad – *Educreations* (free), *Explain Everything* (paid)
  - Android – *Lensoo Create* (free)
- QR Reader of choice
  - Suggested Apps
    - i-nigma
    - Scan
- Website of choice to generate QR codes
  - Suggested websites
    - Qrstuff.com
    - Kaywa

ROOM SET-UP
- Teacher has access to an LCD projector connected a to computer/laptop or
- Teacher has an ipad or tablet, or a classroom set of tablets
- Wi-fi or Apple TV

IN THIS CHAPTER
- Manage a Class Set of Tablets
- Create and Manage Digital Student Portfolios
- Activities Using Tablets Only
  - Rhythm Dictation and Improvisation
  - Melody Dictation and Improvisation
- Create and Use Templates for Lesson Activities and Assessments
- Create and Use Flashcards
- Working with Computers and Tablets
  - Vocal Exploration Activity
  - Sample Kindergarten Activity using Graphic Notation
  - Tracing, Pitch and Rhythm Activities, and Digital Flashcards
  - Send Templates and Images to Tablets/Generate QR Codes
  - Record and Save Student Work

MANAGE A CLASS SET OF TABLETS

Creating a common account for the class set of tablets facilitates downloading of apps. Apps then downloaded to one tablet, can simultaneously be downloaded to all the other devices with the same account.

Numbering the tablets and designating the same tablets to the same students, promotes organization. Students can quickly access, retrieve and continue their work.

Digital Student Portfolios

The greatest advantage of storing student work in a digital portfolio is the ability to retrieve and replay their assessments or activities with ease. The digital portfolio also decreases the use of paper and folders.

Create Student Portfolios via Dropbox or Google Drive

Dropbox and Google Drive Apps may be downloaded onto the tablets. Choose one of the apps to store student work.
- Create a common account.
- Create individual class folders.
- In each of the class folders, create individual student subfolders.
- If the number of students is too great for an individual to create student subfolders, take a few minutes initially in each class to walk students through the Dropbox/ Google app.

• Have students access the Dropbox/Google app, find their class folder, then have them create their own subfolders. This is the folder to which they will upload their work.

Whiteboard Apps

Whiteboard Applications provide opportunities to write and draw on digital paper. The apps range from simple to complex. The simplest whiteboard app has basic tools like a small palette of colors, pencil tool, eraser, redo and undo options, the ability to record audio and screen work simultaneously, options to import images from photo gallery, and access to the camera. The more complex apps have a variety of background templates, extensive color palette, text options, pen options and the ability to import audio, video, PDF files and photos in addition to camera access.

In this chapter, three whiteboard apps will be referenced: *Lensoo Create* (Android), *Educreations* (iPad) and *Explain Everything* (iPad and Android).

Example of a simple whiteboard app: *Educreations* for iPad

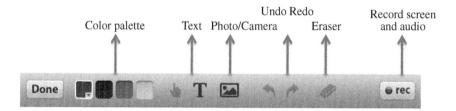

ACTIVITIES USING TABLETS ONLY

Rhythmic Dictation and Improvisation
- Project a tablet using a VGA adapter, Apple TV, or Reflector app.
- Walk students through the basic tools of the whiteboard app if using it for the very first time.
- For younger students, creating a form or box template to write or draw their answers in may be helpful.
- Ask students to choose a color and draw a line first vertically then horizontally across the page, thus creating 4 boxes. Help them number the boxes to keep track to their work.
- Once students have mastered writing on the tablet, more boxes may be added.
- Using rhythm syllables of choice, administer the dictation activity.
- **Example for Quarter and Eighth Notes and Quarter Rest using *Educreations***

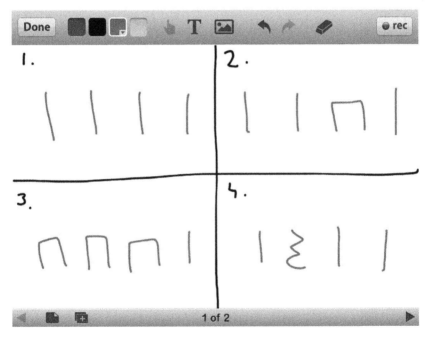

- Have students repeat the dictation by speaking and/or clapping or playing on un-pitched percussion.
- Have them record their performance, and save it on the tablets.
- They may upload these into their own student folders in Dropbox or Google Drive.
- **Composition Extension:** Individual or small groups of students may write, speak and play, and record their own 16-beat composition.

Melodic Dictation and Improvisation

- Project a tablet using a VGA adapter, Apple TV, or Reflector app.
- Walk students through the steps of setting up a template for the activity.
- Have students imitate the steps of opening the app.
- The example shown here is a basic dictation with two pitches, *so-mi,* using *Explain Everything.*
- For younger children, start by just having them draw two parallel lines as best they can with the pen tool.

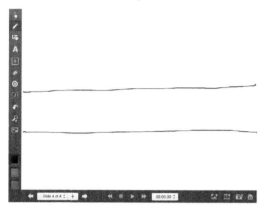

- Sing the pitches, and have students write them down.

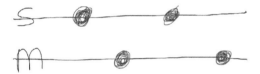

- When students get more comfortable using the app, they can insert lines and shapes using the shape tools.

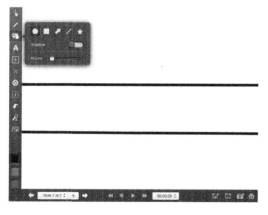

- The Lock function can be used to lock the lines, so that they will not move as students are drawing on the screen.

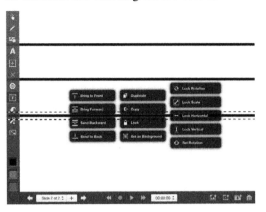

- Once students are comfortable navigating the basic functions of the apps, the dictations and assessments may become longer and more sophisticated.
- Example of 4-measure melodic dictation

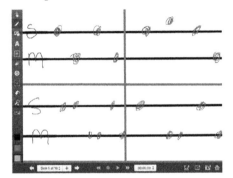

- Example of singing and recording melodic contour

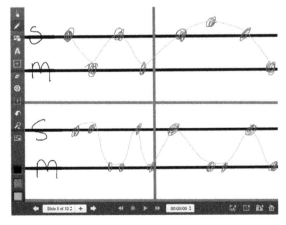

- Students can be given prescribed rhythms, and asked to create melodies using known pitches.

- Melodic dictation for treble staff may be administered by giving students words to spell, or by writing/displaying the notes on a whiteboard and having the students copy, then solve the treble staff note names to spell out the words.

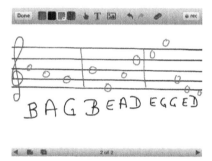

CREATE TEMPLATES IN TABLETS FOR ACTIVITIES AND ASSESSMENTS

Some whiteboard apps, like *Explain Everything*, have more than the basic tools of Text, Pen, Eraser and Record. A Whiteboard app that has the ability to incorporate lines and shapes can be used to create templates for a variety of activities.

Templates may be created on a tablet, saved to the photo browser and pushed to other tablets via email, Dropbox, Google drive or QR codes.

Some examples are as follows.

Box Templates

Box templates are a great aid. They are simple to create but have multiple uses.

- In *Explain Everything*, choose a color, then the Line tool from the Shapes menu.

- Draw lines to divide the screen into required sections.

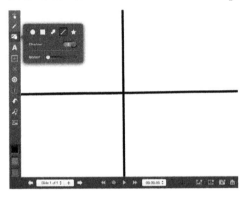

- Number the boxes if needed. This can be an aid in dictation and composition activities.

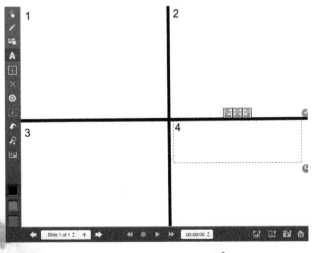

- Here is an example of a more sophisticated template of a table that uses a rectangle, divided into boxes by lines or by duplicating multiple boxes to create the template.

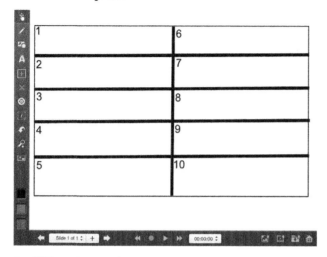

- Staff Templates with 2 to 5 lines: Multiple lines can be drawn, using the Shapes tool, to create 2 to 5-line staves.

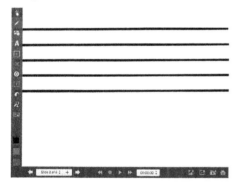

- Using the Shapes and Text tools, the staves may be further customized to include notating selected solfege pitches.

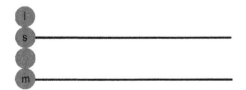

Create Templates and Worksheets from Templates

- Once templates are created, they may be saved in the photo browser by clicking on the Picture Frame icon on the bottom right hand corner of the screen.

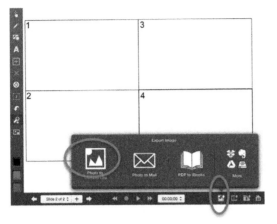

- The following is an example of how to create various kinds of worksheets using the 5-line staff template that was saved to the Photo Browser.

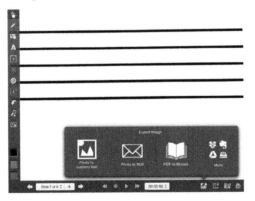

- Open a new project in *Explain Everything*, Click the Plus Sign icon to Insert an Existing Photo/Video.

- Choose the 5-line staff from the Camera Roll.

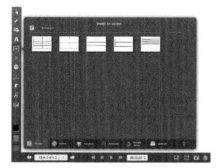

- Once inserted, the picture automatically opens in the Edit Image page. Crop the image if desired, and click Done.

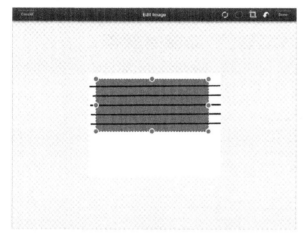

- Once the image is on the screen, it maybe duplicated using the "I" icon.

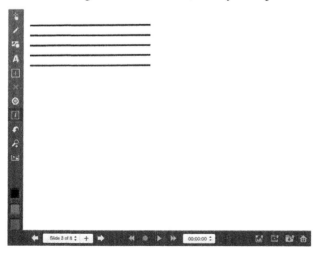

- Tap the Icon then the Object for the menu to appear, then select Duplicate.

- Using the Text tool, write out words that students can spell on the treble staff and save the worksheet as a picture.

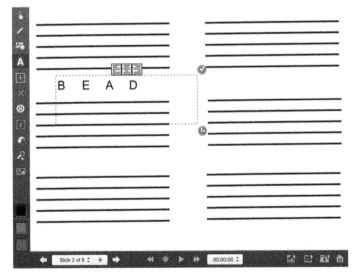

- Or dictate words that students first write under each staff, then draw the notes.
- Or draw notes on the staff for students to spell out the note names below.

- The following is an example of three different ways a simple template may be used.

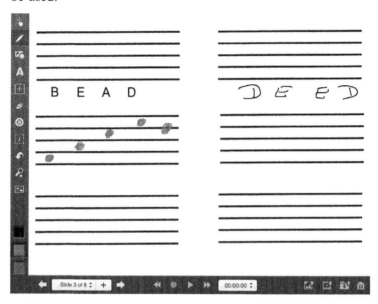

CREATE RHYTHM FLASHCARDS (in *Explain Everything*)

- Using the Shape tool, first draw a circle, then a line. Arrange them to form a quarter note. Tap the junction of the two objects three times. They will then be grouped and move as one object. Use the "I" icon, and tap on the quarter note. Use the Duplicate option to replicate the quarter note.

- Save the image to the Camera Roll, by clicking the Picture Frame icon on the bottom right hand side of the screen.
- Create multiple 2, 3, or 4-beat flashcards.

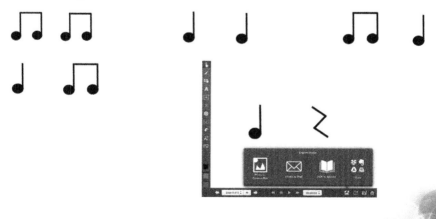

- Once the worksheets, templates, and flashcards are created, they may be pushed onto Student tablets by emailing them to the common tablet email, or they may be uploaded to the shared Google Drive or Dropbox folder to be downloaded by students.
- Note that these templates need to be downloaded just one time onto student tablets. Once they reside in the Photo Browser or Camera Roll, the templates may be used by multiple students.

WORKING WITH COMPUTERS AND TABLETS

Vocal Exploration Activity: Movement – Computer –Tablet

Movement

A simple vocal warm-up with children involves throwing a scarf up in the air, tracking its path downwards while vocalizing on a pre-assigned vocable, like "whee", or "whoo".

- Students stop vocalizing once the scarf touches the floor. An extension of this would be to have students physically mirror a pathway that the teacher describes in the air with the scarf.
- The activity may be repeated with student leaders, culminating in students drawing their pathways on paper and either demonstrating to or conducting the class by dragging their finger across the pathway.

Computer

- Using PowerPoint or Word or IWB applications, one can create and edit images and pathways for vocal exploration.
- Using the animation features in PowerPoint, students may vocally track a snowflake swirling in the wind, a bee buzzing from flower to flower, a witch on a broomstick flying around a bonfire or in search of her cauldron of witch's brew!

Tablet

- The same images of objects and pathways may be sent to iPads/tablets via Dropbox, email, or QR codes. Please see **Instructions to access computer generated templates and images to iPads or Tablets** (p. 50).
- Images may be accessed in the photo browser of the iPads. Students then access the *Educreations* app on their iPads.
- The class model is demonstrated on the class Screen.
- They are walked through accessing the primary object (snowflake, bat, owl, or witch), inserting and resizing the image into the app, and placing it on the top, middle or bottom left of the screen.

- They do the same for the pre-selected pathway. They can then drag the object along the pathway while vocalizing.

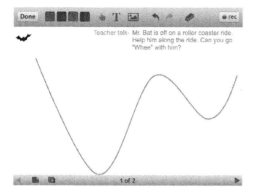

- They can record their voice and their action on screen, and play it back for themselves or each other.

- Later they can draw their own pathways for the object across the screen.
- They can do this activity in pairs or in small groups, with students creating pathways for each other, performing, recording, assessing and providing constructive feedback.
- This activity can take from 5 -10 minutes, depending on the lesson objective.

Sample Kindergarten Activity using *Educreations*

- After kindergarten students have experienced internal and external steady beat activities, they may enjoy the following graphic notation activity on the their Tablet.
- In *Educreations*, students may select two colors, one to indicate sounds with a beat and another for sounds without a beat.
- The music selection for this activity may be a pre-recorded sample with snippets of classical or pop music, alternating with sounds like wind chimes, siren, wind in the trees etc. with recorded in pauses.
- However, a hand drum and a wind chime may be used toward the same objective.

45

- Students tap the steady beat on the tablet in accompaniment to the teacher's drumming.
- When the teacher pauses, they may choose another color and create a swirl to the wind chimes played by the teacher.
- If it is an assessment, the activity may be recorded by pressing the record button.
- Students may then playback their work, and see if their strokes kept time with the music.
- The teacher can also review their work at anytime, then or later.

Tracing, Worksheets and Digital Flashcards

- Use the Shapes tools and the dotted line options to create note heads, stems, flags and beams.
- Students may trace these on the IWB or on their iPads to draw notes.
- Similarly, worksheets may be created to be completed on iPads. These are great activities for substitute teachers!

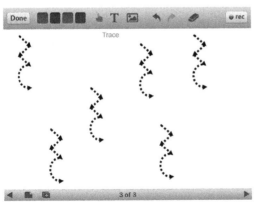

- The 2, 4, and 3-beat rhythm (stick and regular notation) and melodic flashcards may be created using PowerPoint, Word or IWB applications.

- Students access these flashcards on their iPads to create rhythmic and melodic compositions that are extended to movement, Orff instruments and recorders.
- Working in small groups, they can use these flashcards to create, record and assess their compositions. The teacher now has digital portfolios for each student that are easily retrievable for review, for assessment, during parent conferences, and for grading purposes.

The following are some examples of student work using images and templates sent to the tablets. These may be digitally recorded using the Record functions, saved as Screencasts and archived.

- 4-Box Template in *Educreations*

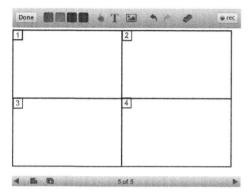

- 16-beat student rhythm composition in *Explain Everything* using the 4-box template.

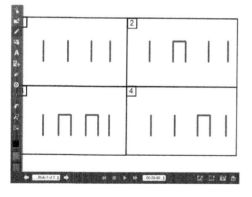

- Student-created composition in *Explain Everything*, using 2-beat rhythm flashcards and the 4-box template.

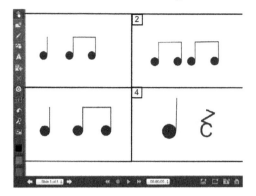

- Student-created melodic composition in *Explain Everything*, using 4-beat *so-mi-la* flashcards and the 4-box template.

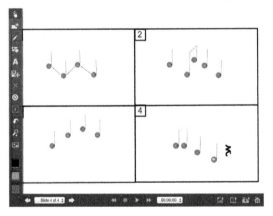

- Student composition using a *so-mi* staff and a prescribed rhythm template.

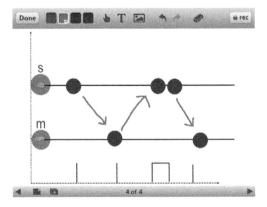

- *Mi-re-do* melodic composition in *Explain Everything*, using 3-line staff and rhythm template.

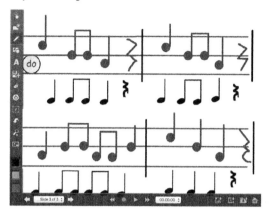

- Small group-created pattern, that will be played on sticks and drums using movement

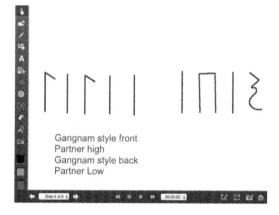

Gangnam style front
Partner high
Gangnam style back
Partner Low

Instructions to access computer-generated templates and images to iPads or Tablets

If a class cart of iPads or Tablets is available, creating a common account for the tablets will facilitate downloading apps. If an app is downloaded on one tablet, the common account facilitates it being downloaded on to all. This avoids downloading apps onto individual tablets.

Create a common email address for all iPads or Tablets. This allows documents or files to be sent to all the tablets simultaneously.

Images, or PDFs saved as images, may be accessed on the tablet in many ways.

3 ways to send an image file to an iPad or tablet. (Use what is easiest for you.)

1. Email
- Email the image file using the common email address.
- Instruct students to access the mail app and open the specified email.
- On iPads, click Reply to access the dropdown menu. One of the options is Save Images.
- Save the file on the iPad or tablet.

2. QR Codes
- Use a QR generator to create a QR code for the image file. Ensure that the image has been saved in a place like Dropbox, or Google Drive, or elsewhere where a link can be shared by the students. Use a QR generator website and follow the instructions described on the site to generate QR codes for the images.
- QR codes may be individually accessed by each tablet using a QR reader app (free app download), and saved if needed on the tablet.

3. Dropbox: A Dropbox account may be set up on the website **dropbox.com**. A Dropbox account may be created using the common email address for the tablets. The Dropbox app may then be downloaded onto the tablets. Images can be uploaded to the Dropbox account by the teacher, and downloaded onto the tablets by the students by accessing the Dropbox on the tablets.

Note: A similar procedure may be used with Google Drive.

Once the image files have been sent to the tablets and saved in the Dropbox or Photo app, they may be accessed and imported into iPad or Android apps, such as *Educreations* or *Explain Everything*. These apps allow image files to be written or drawn upon, so that players can mark their own Bingo cards. Some of these apps also include a record function for assessment or other instructional purpose.

Import a saved image file in *Educreations*
- Open the *Educreations* app. Look for a Picture Frame on the top menu bar.
- Tap the picture to view the dropdown menu.

- Search for the required image.

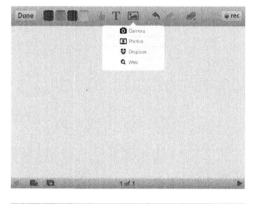

- Tap on the image to insert it into the *Educreations* page.
- Manipulate the image as required.

Record Student Work

- Ask students to click the Record button for assessment or other instructional purpose.

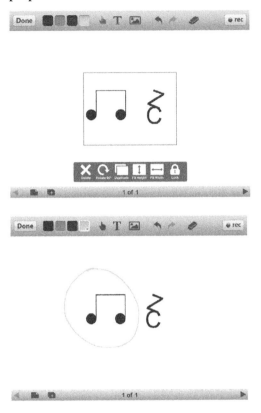

Save Student Work in *Educreations*

- Student work can be saved as Screencasts on the iPad, or shared on a website under a private pre-created teacher account, or uploaded to Dropbox or Google drive. They may be emailed to the teacher.

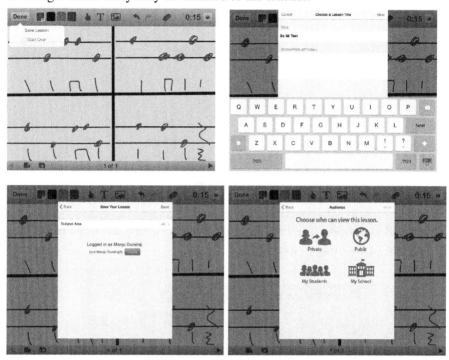

There is an option to Copy Lesson Link, that allows the Screencast to be accessed privately or publicly on the *Educreations* website under the Teacher's account.

Save Student Work in *Explain Everything*

- Students can save their work by clicking the Home icon at the bottom right hand corner of the screen, and using the options directed by the teacher.

- The work may be saved as a PDF or as an image. Recorded work may be saved as a video. The varied options include saving in Dropbox or Google Drive or emailing to the teacher.

CHAPTER 3

Interactive Whiteboards (IWBs)

HARDWARE
- LCD Projector
- Laptop/Desktop computer
- Interactive Whiteboard

SOFTWARE
- Notebook application, if using SMART Board
- ActiveInspire, if using Promethean Board

ROOM SET-UP
Teacher has access to an LCD projector connected to a computer/laptop connected to the IWB.

PRIOR KNOWLEDGE
- Accessing the IWB application on the computer
- Connecting and Orienting the IWB
- At least a rudimentary knowledge of tools in IWB software

IN THIS CHAPTER
- Tools
- Create and Trace Notes and Rests
- Fade In Animation: Label Parts of a Note
- Fade Out Animation: Identify Silent Beat and Eighth Note
  - Pease Porridge Hot
- Extensions: Recognizing Form and Rhythm Composition
- Create an Animated Xylophone
- Create an Interactive Solfege Ladder
- Visualize the Connection between Xylophone and Solfege Ladder
- Create an Animated Recorder
- Export Images to Tablets

SMART BOARD TOOLS

Although this chapter references SMART Notebook software, similar tools and functions will appear in the software for other IWBs.

SMART Notebook has a clear user-friendly interface.

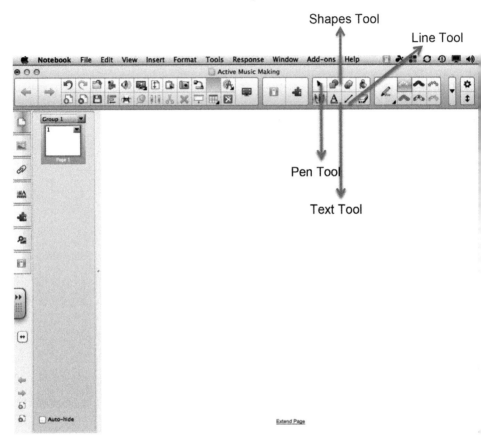

Tools

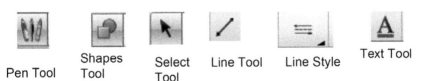

Pen Tool   Shapes Tool   Select Tool   Line Tool   Line Style   Text Tool

Content Gallery

It is important to know that objects that are created and will be used frequently may be saved in the Content Gallery for repeated use. Create subfolders in the Content Gallery to organize these images.

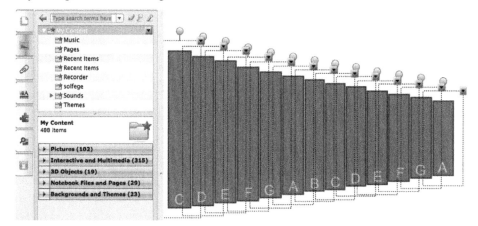

Create a subfolder by clicking on the drop down arrow of the Content Gallery and selecting New Folder that may be named.

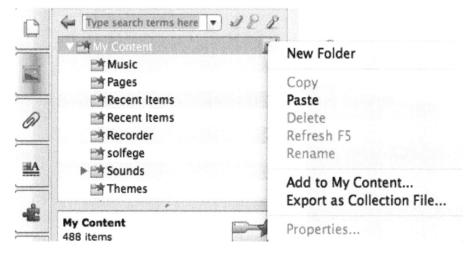

CREATE AND TRACE NOTES AND RESTS

Notehead

 Shapes

- Using the Shapes tool, select the Circle from the contextual menu.

Shapes   Circle

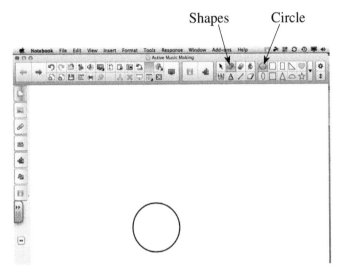

- Use the Select tool to select the Circle. When an object is selected, a blue dotted square appears around it.

 Select

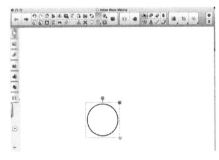

- Select the Line Style tool and select the Dotted Line style and desired thickness.

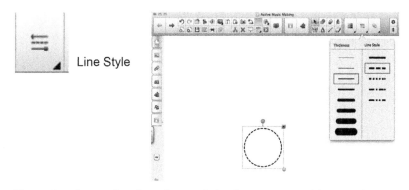

Line Style

- For a simple notehead tracing activity for younger children, duplicate the dotted circle by clicking the black arrow that reveals the dropdown menu. Select the Clone option, and make as many copies as needed.

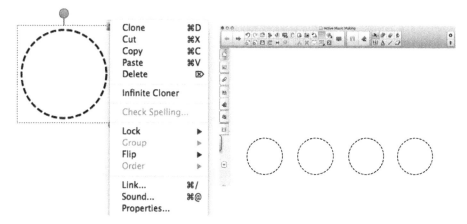

- If using this with students for a tracing activity for whole notes or note-heads, ask students to select a pen from the Pen Tray, or choose a color from the Pen Tools Contextual menu.

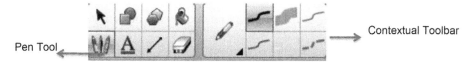

Pen Tool

Contextual Toolbar

- Ask students to trace the circles if practicing tracing whole notes or trace and color in the circles if practicing drawing noteheads.

Half, Quarter and Eighth Notes

- To create half, quarter and eighth notes, follow the same steps to create a circle.

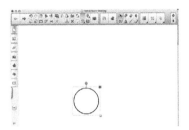

- Select a line from the Line Tool contextual toolbar.

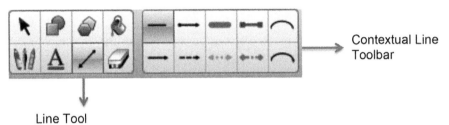

Contextual Line Toolbar

Line Tool

- Draw a line from the circle.

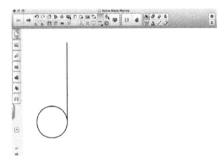

- Group the objects in any of the following three ways:
  - Select the line and the circle by using the Select Tool. Click outside the area of the objects and drag so that the area covering the objects is covered. This Marquee selection ensures all objects in the area are selected.

- Another way to select multiple objects is hold down the Shift Key while clicking on each object.

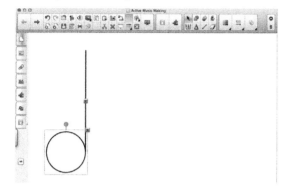

- A third option is to click on any of the arrows to reveal the drop down menu. Select the Group option to group objects into one.

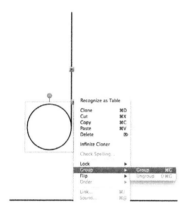 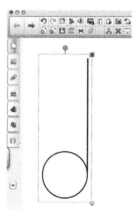

- In case the note is to be used for tracing activities, the Line Style can be changed by selecting the object and choosing the desired option from the Line Style sub-menu.

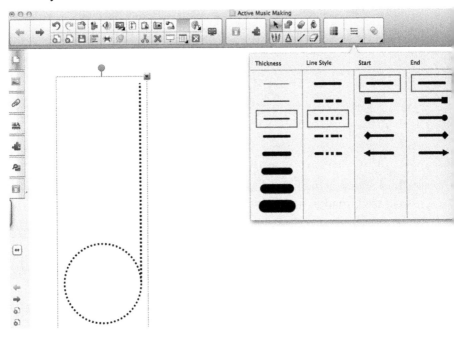

- This can then be duplicated using the Clone option (Command D – on macs).

Eighth Note

- To create an eighth note, select the curve from the Line Tool contextual menu.

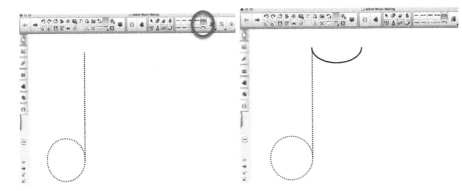

- Select the curve. Use the green circle to rotate the curve to the desired position and angle. If using for tracing, change the Line Style to dotted line.

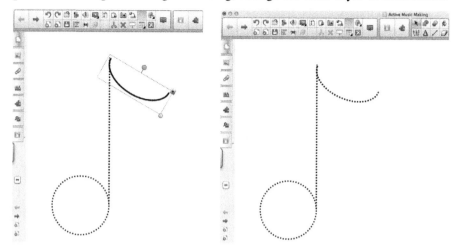

- If creating two eighth notes that are beamed, duplicate the note without the curve, draw a line to connect the stems, and change the Line Style to dotted. Group the line and the notes to create beamed eighth notes.

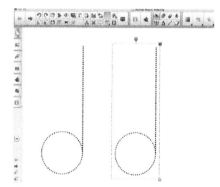
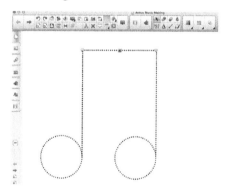

- Once the notes are grouped and selected to form one object, they may be resized and duplicated to form a worksheet. Use the grey circle to resize the selected object.

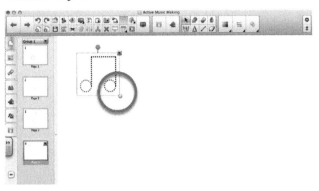

Quarter Rest

- A quarter rest maybe created using lines, and a curve. Using arrow heads will help students practice drawing rests correctly while tracing.

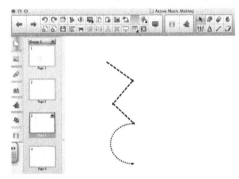

- Each note or rest created may be copied and pasted onto the same or different pages page using Copy and Paste functions similar to those in word.

Sample Worksheet

- Here is a sample of a worksheet that may be done on the IWB, printed out or sent to tablets.

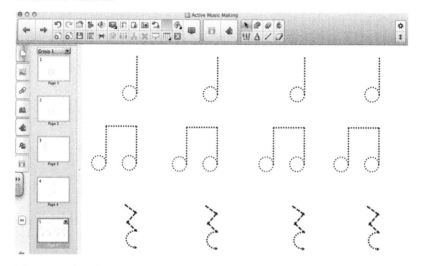

- The completed worksheet would look like this.

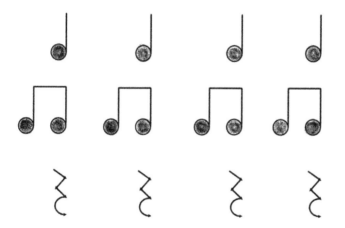

FADE IN ANIMATION: LABEL PARTS OF A NOTE

This labeling activity demonstrates the Fade In Animation tool in SMART Notebook.
- Use the dotted line from Line Style tool, with the Arrow. Select the lines and Lock them so they stay in place.

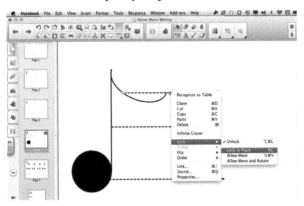

- Use the Shapes tool to draw rectangular boxes.

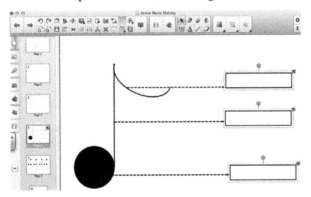

- Select all the boxes, using the marquee selection, or hold down the shift key while clicking on them. Select a Line color and a Fill color for the boxes. Lock the boxes so they don't move when touched.

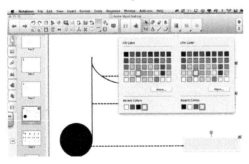

- Choose the Text Tool, select the desired color and font from the Contextual Menu, type in the answers, and position the text in the correct boxes.

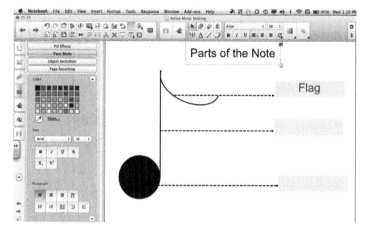

- Select all the answers. Each of these may be animated separately, but if there are multiple objects that will need the same animation, it is quicker to do them in one step.
- Click on any of the down arrows on any selected objects, and select the Properties option. Alternatively the Properties option on the sidebar may be used, but all the objects to be animated need to be selected.

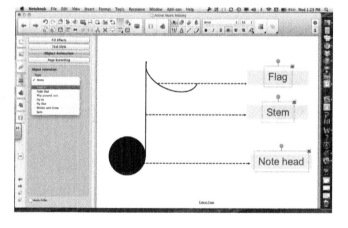

- Select the Object Animation option, and select the kind of Object Animation desired.

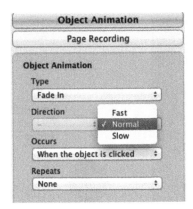

- Ensure that these objects are Locked, so that they do not move around when tapped. Choose the drop down arrow menu for the Lock option.

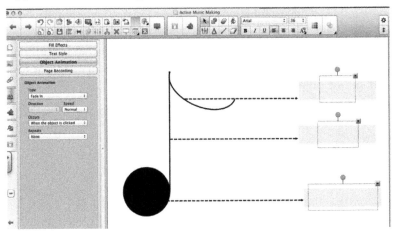

- Create a Heading to add style to the visual.

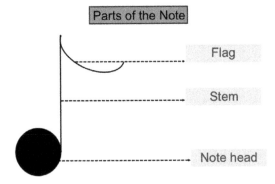

- It is easier to draw a box, using the Rectangle option from the Shapes menu. Fill it in with the Color and Line style desired. Type the Text and place it in the box. Group and Lock the objects.

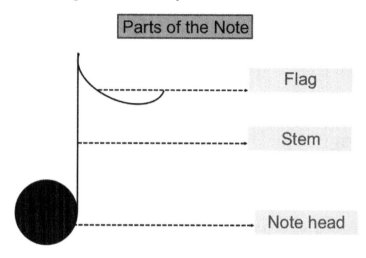

- However if the Text is typed first, and a box created afterward, the box will appear in front of the text.

- Select the box, then the drop down arrow on the box, click on Order and select Send to Back. Fill in the box colors before or after doing this.

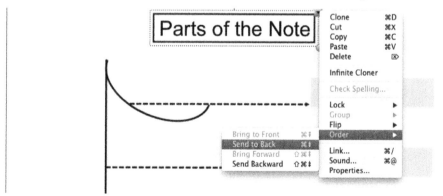

- When presenting to the class, the page will look like this.

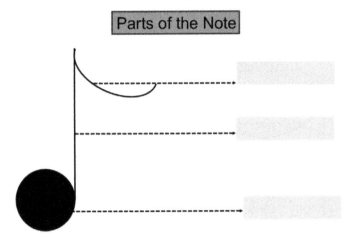

- When the boxes are tapped, the answers will appear.

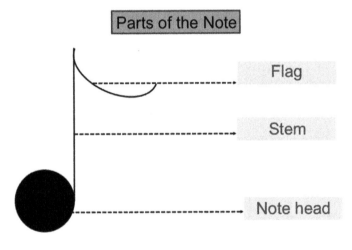

- To increase interactivity, students may write in their answers on the dotted lines and check by tapping the boxes; or boxes may be created for student answers, that may be checked by tapping answer boxes.

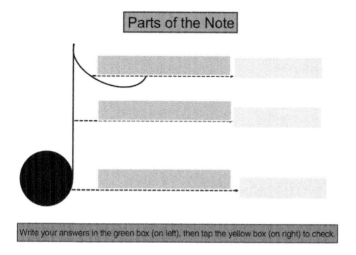

FADE OUT: IDENTIFY SILENT BEAT AND EIGHTH NOTE

The lesson process in this activity is reflected in the visuals presented to the class.

Process Possibility
- Students speak/read the poem.
- Students pat the steady beat.
- Students identify where the silent beat occurs.
- Students identify where there are two sounds on the beat (the eighth notes occur).
- Students play the rhythm using body percussion, then un-pitched percussion.
- Students create a B section using 2-beat digital flashcards.
- Students choose the form of the piece.
- Students perform.

Visual Presentation

Create Page 1: Text page
- Using the text tool, type out the text of the poem in a text box.

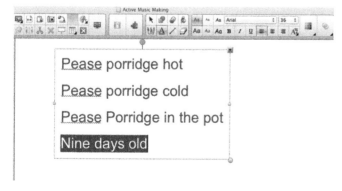

- Select each line, Click and Drag it out of the text box.

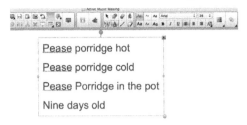

Pease porridge hot

Pease porridge cold

Pease Porridge in the pot

Nine days old

- Space each line of text as desired.

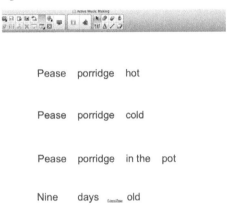

Pease   porridge   hot

Pease   porridge   cold

Pease   porridge   in the   pot

Nine   days   ____ old

Create Page 2

- Insert a new page using the Add Page, Copy and Paste the text, or simply Clone the page by selecting the drop down menu from the Page Sorter.

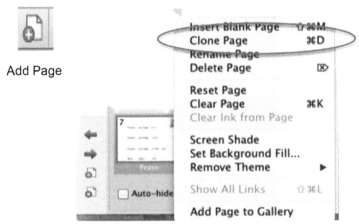

Add Page

Insert Blank Page	⇧⌘M
Clone Page	⌘D
Rename Page	
Delete Page	⌦
Reset Page	
Clear Page	⌘K
Clear Ink from Page	
Screen Shade	
Set Background Fill...	
Remove Theme	▶
Show All Links	⇧⌘L
Add Page to Gallery	

- SMART Notebook includes a Gallery of images that may be downloaded/ installed at the same the Notebook application is installed.

Gallery Tab

Use the Gallery icon on the sidebar and type in "bowl". Double-click on the image to insert it onto the page.

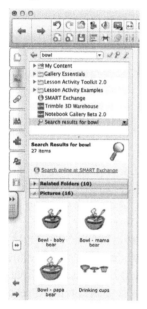

- Duplicate the 'bowl' using the Clone option. Since each bowl represents a beat, place it above the text where the beat occurs.
- Use the Alignment Guides to ensure the bowls and texts are neatly placed. If the Guide tool does not appear on the Top Menu bar, drag it in from the Settings tab, which is the little gear on the top right hand side of the page.

- Select all the 4 bowls in the first line and Copy and Paste them onto subsequent lines. Page 2 now visually shows the beats (bowls) and silent beats – bowls with no text below.

- Clone Page 2 (for Page 3) before selecting all the objects and Locking them. This helps student or teacher to tap the bowls on the Smart Board without them moving away.

Create Page 3

- On Page 3, students need to identify the Silent beats/rests by tapping the bowls with no text. To create a graphic for the silent beat, insert a clipart image for a little puff of smoke, or create 3 circles stacked on top of each other, group them together and fill them with a smoky grey color.
- Place these on top of the Silent Beat bowls.

- Select all 3 smoke puffs, and click on any one of the drop down arrows. Select Order, and Send to Back. These will put the puffs behind the bowls.

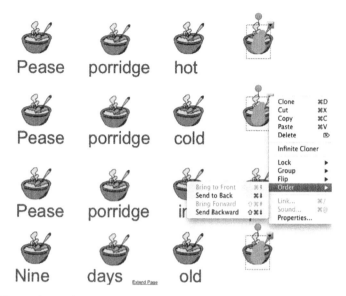

- Keep the puffs selected, click on any of the drop down arrows and Lock in Place.

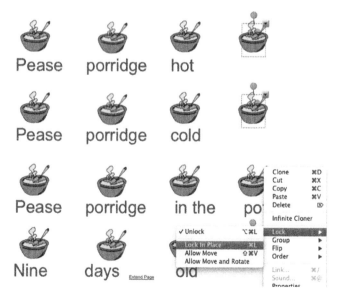

- The puffs are behind the bowls. Select the Silent beat bowls, click on the drop down arrow for Properties, and select Object Animation.

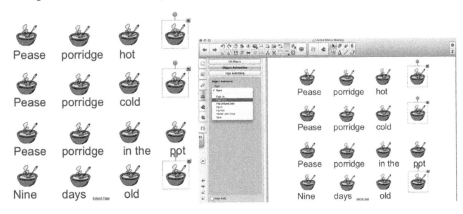

- Select the Fade Out Animation. Ensure it occurs When Object is clicked. Lock the bowls in place once animation is done. When bowls are clicked, they will Fade Out, revealing the puffs!

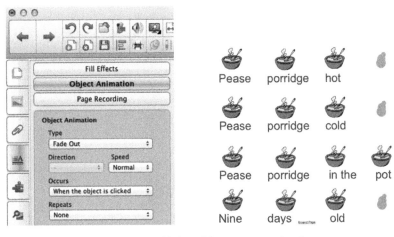

- Clone the Page, to ensure all the objects appear in the same way on the next page.

Create Page 4

- The objective on Page 4 is to create two smaller bowls that represent two sounds on the beat. These are to be sized to fit inside a bigger bowl. Insert a bowl from the Gallery, or copy and resize a bowl using the grey sizing circle that appears when the object is selected.

- Duplicate the small bowl and Group them together.

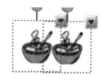

- Place these over the bowls that have 2 sounds on the beat –"porridge", "in the".

- Select these little bowls and Send them to the Back of the bigger bowls using the drop down arrow. Then Lock them in Place while they are still selected.

- Select the bigger bowl in front of the smaller ones. Use the drop down arrow menu to select Properties. Use the Fade Out object animation. Select all the objects and Lock them in place.

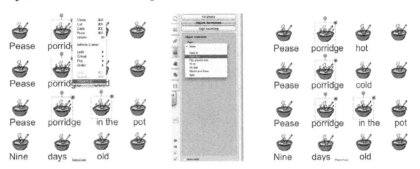

- When clicked, the animated page will look like this.

Create Page 5

- Clone Page 4. Remove all the animation by Unlocking all the objects, and removing the animations from each. A quick way to do this is to go to the Edit menu in the Top Tool bar, Select All Locked Objects, click on one of the Locks and unlock. Every object on the page will be unlocked.

- Thus far, graphic representations of the quarter rest and eighth notes have been created. Regular notation may also be used instead of the Graphic notation, by clicking the Gallery tab in the side bar, then clicking the Gallery Essentials folder, selecting the Arts folder, and then the Music subfolder. Under Pictures, there will appear a variety of music notes.

- ▪ Double-click the quarter note and eighth notes to insert them onto the page. They can then be Duplicated and placed over the respective bowls.
- ▪ In case Notes of choice are not found in the Gallery, create them using the Shapes and Line Tools.

- Select all the notes and rests and Send them to the Back, then Lock these in Place.

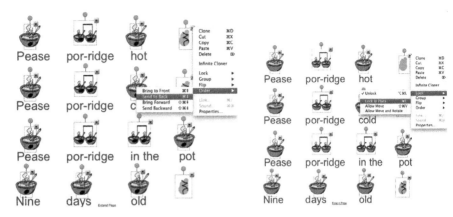

- Select all the bowls and smoke puffs, use the drop down arrow to select Properties. Choose the Object Animation panel on the side bar, and select the Fade Out option. Lock all objects in place.
- When the animation is applied, the page will look like this.

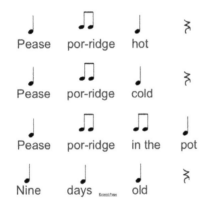

Completed Visual Presentation

Page 1

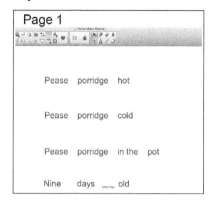

Page 2: Tap the Beat

Page 3: Identify Silent Beat

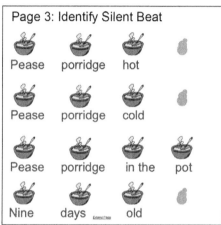

Page 4: Identify 2 Sounds

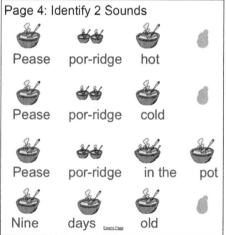

Page 5: Adding Notation

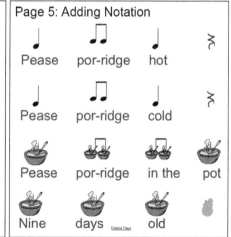

EXTENSION 1: RECOGNIZING FORM

Extend lesson to help students identify same and different patterns.

- Using the Shapes tool, draw rectangular boxes, and place the rhythm of the poem in them. Draw smaller Answer boxes on the side.

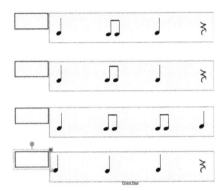

- Add Text – **Same**, **Different**, **Variation** on the bottom of the page. Since the first two lines of the poem are the same, use the Infinite Cloner option in the drop down arrow menu of the text **Same**.

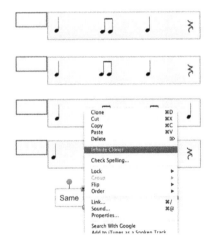

• Students can drag the answers to the correct boxes.

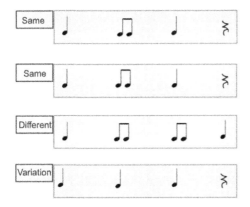

EXTENSION 2: RHYTHM COMPOSITION

• Give students the opportunity to create their own B Section – a 16-beat rhythm composition, with the rhythm of the poem being the A section.
• Draw 4 boxes for the A section; Group them; Select them and choose desired Line and Fill colors.
• Repeat the above for the B section.

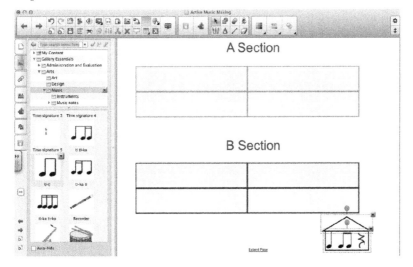

- From the Music subfolder in the Arts folder in the Gallery Essentials folder in the Gallery, drag out quarter note, rest and eighth notes. Place them on the page, select all of them, click the drop down menu and select Infinite Cloner.

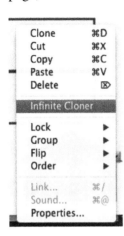

- Students can drag the notes into the boxes.
- To make the page look more professional in appearance, create a little Note House for the notes, using the rectangle and triangle options from the Shapes toolbar.
- To aid students, put the Form vocabulary words "Same" "Different" "Variation" in another house.

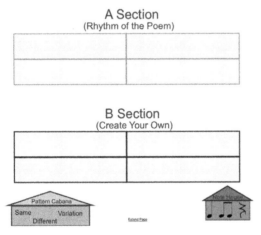

- Students can create their own patterns first using the class model, then in small groups.
- They may perform their compositions as a Rondo, using body percussion or un-pitched instruments.
- They may even transfer the rhythm composition to barred instruments set up in a pentatonic pattern.

CREATE AN ANIMATED XYLOPHONE

The process of creating a Xylophone in SMART Notebook is very similar to the one in PowerPoint. It may initially take a while, but once created, it may be used in many ways and forms. It will be worthwhile to create Xylophone Templates that may be used over and over again, and adapted to the lesson situation.

For example:

Original Xylophone

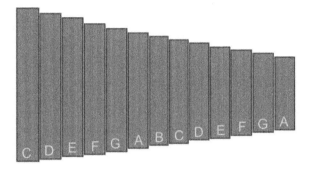

Boomwhacker Xylophone

Create

- Using the Shapes tool, draw a rectangle. Use the color palette to select Line color and Fill color.

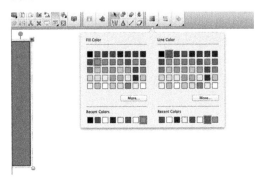

- Duplicate this rectangle 12 times, and resize the boxes so that there 13 rectangles.

Tip: Drag the duplicates over the previous box and resize using the first box as a mold. This ensures that the boxes are even in width.

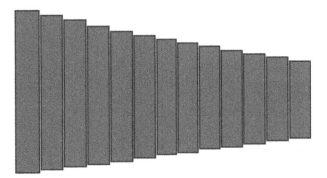

- To create a Xylophone that matches Boomwhacker colors, select each bar and fill in the appropriate color from the color palette.

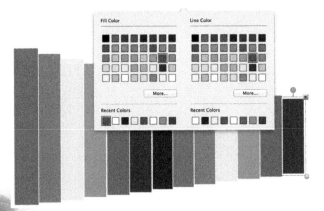

- Use the Text tool to type the letter names C, D, E, F, G, A, C, D, E, F, G, A.

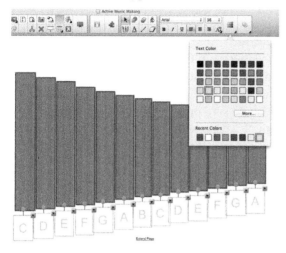

- Place each letter name on its corresponding bar and Group the Text and the rectangle using the drop down arrow menu.

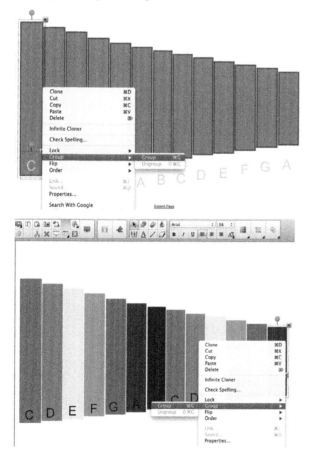

Once these xylophones are made, save the pages in a separate file. These xylophones may be copied and manipulated in many ways.

Create a Pentatonic Xylophone

- To set up a visual for the Xylophone in C pentatonic where C is *do*, the F and B bars need to be removed The *fa* and *ti* bars may be set to Fly Off the screen on touch/click, so that only the *do, re, mi, so, la* bars remain. This is an effective visual for students to sing or to set up their instruments.
- Select the "F", "B" and high "F" bars on the xylophone. The animation may be done individually or collectively by holding down the Shift key and clicking the necessary bars.

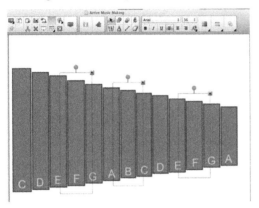

- Access the Object Animation menu, by choosing Properties in the drop down arrow menu.

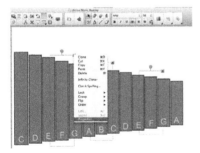
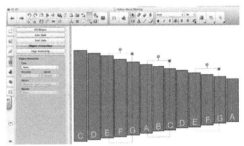

Select Fly Out or Fade Out. If selecting the former, additional options include Flying Out from any direction. Choose the desired direction (for example, "top") and speed ("slow").

- While the bars are selected, choose the Lock option from the drop down arrow menu, and select the Allow Move option. This allows the bars to move without the objects getting Ungrouped.

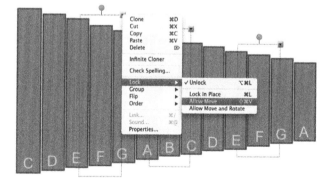

- When the bars are touched, or clicked on the computer, they will Fly Off.

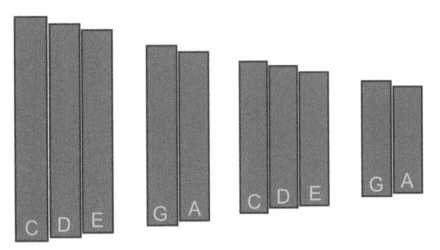

Add Solfege

If students need to see the connection between solfege letter names or the diatonic scale, create a Text pattern *d,r,m,f,s,l,t,d'*, then space the text so that they match up with the bars. Group the text together like the following example.

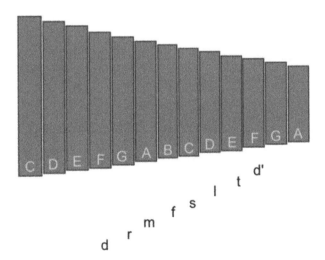

This movable *do* graphic can be moved across the Xylophone to demonstrate, that while the actual pitch letter names remain the same, their solfege names change depending on which pitch is *do*. For example, *do* = F.

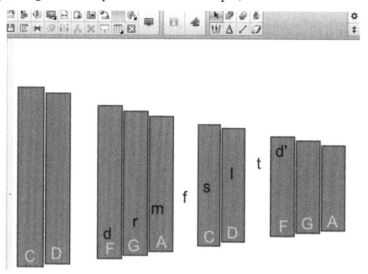

- To demonstrate a connection between solfege names, hand signs and letter names, either draw or search online for hand signs. Group each hand sign to its solfege name. Space and then group the text and hand signs into one object.

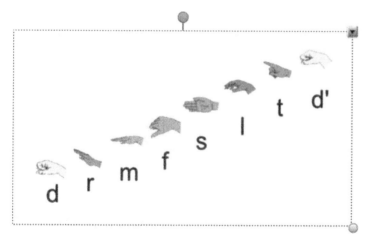

- Now this pattern can be dragged over the xylophone bars to be a powerful visual for students.

Note: It will also be worthwhile to animate all the bars to Fly Off. This Xylophone page may be duplicated and used many times, allowing any of the bars to be removed at any desired moment.

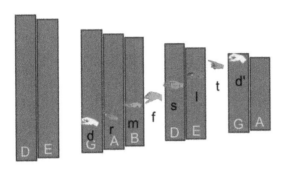

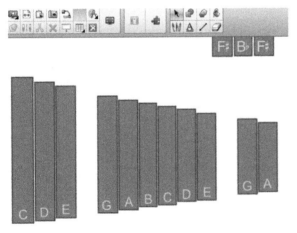

Note: Additional accidental bars – F#s and B♭ – may be created by duplicating the F bars and B bar, and changing the text. These may be used as needed too.

Add Visual Chord Identifiers

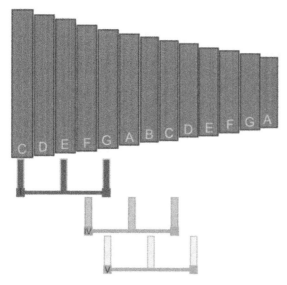

Visual chord identifiers help students visualize triads, identify common pitches in related chords and provide a basis to create melodies.

Pease Porridge Hot Melodic Composition Example

The Xylophone visual may be presented to students as part of the Pease Porridge Presentation. Students can play the rhythm pattern on any pitch set of the teacher's choice. For e.g *so-mi, mi-re-do, so-mi-re-do, la-so-mi-re-do* or the entire pentatonic scale.

They may even experiment starting and ending on *la*, experiencing a *la*-based melody.

CREATE AN INTERACTIVE SOLFEGE LADDER

An interactive solfege ladder may be as visually effective as a one made of cloth or hard board. A basic chart may be created using rectangle and circle shapes, and adding text within the circles.

- Using the Shapes tool, draw a circle and select a Line color

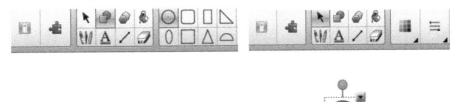

- Duplicate the circle 10 times. Use the Alignment Guide to line each circle precisely under the one above.
- The Alignment Guide tool may be added to the main tool bar by clicking the gear icon.

- Select Show/Hide Alignment and drag the icon to the top left hand side of the top menu bar.

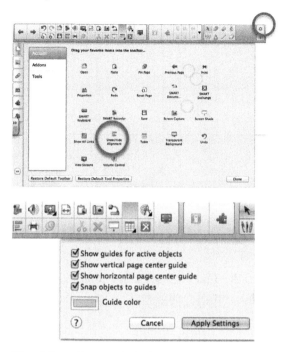

- The Aligned row of circles look like this.

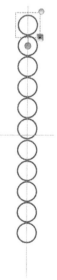

- Use the above un-grouped circles as a template. Duplicate the page, by going into Page Sorter mode and selecting Clone Page.

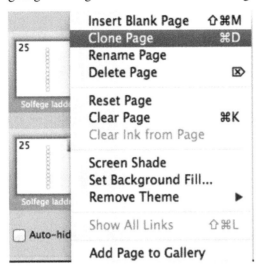

- To add text to the circles, go to the Text tool, select the required font and color. Group each circle with its corresponding text.

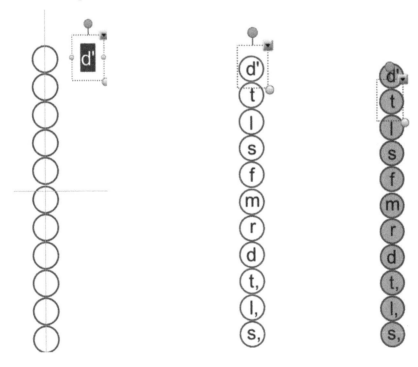

The solfege ladder can be customized then manipulated depending on the purpose. For example:

- If the circles are to be colored in, they can be selected using the Marquee selection – click outside the area and drag across objects to be selected. Choose a color to fill in the circle.
- The circles may also be of different colors if you want to make chord or triad connections.
- If only some pitches need to be revealed at a given time, then all the pitches need to be covered initially.
- Create circles similar in size to the ones that make up the solfege ladder. The circles can be the same color, or different. Ensure that each of these blank circles is filled in with a color.

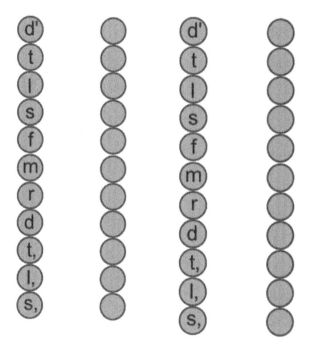

- Select the original solfege ladder and Lock it in Place.

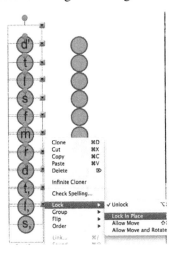

- Click, drag and place a blank circle on top of each of the pitches on the solfege ladder.

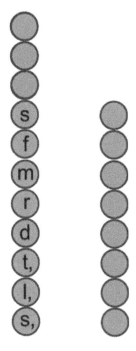

- Once all the blank circles are atop the solfege pitch ladder, select all the blank circles using the Marquee selection. The solfege ladder will not be selected because it is locked.

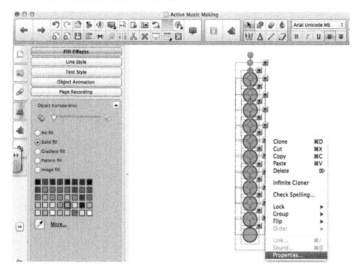

- Select Properties from the drop down menu of any one of the circles.
- From the sidebar, select the Object Animation option. Select Fade Out option.

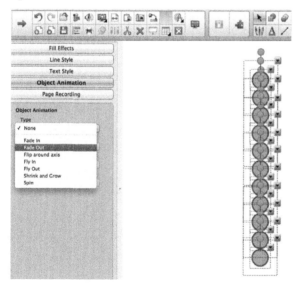

- Now when the required pitches are touched, the covering circle fades out, revealing the pitch below.

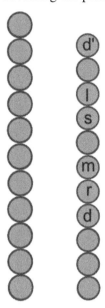

- Alternatively, instead of using the Fade Out animation option, one filled-in circle may be used. Select the Infinite Cloner option from the drop down menu.

- This allows an infinite number of circles to be dragged and placed over pitches that need to be covered.
- Alternatively, a specific number of circles may be cloned and placed over each other.

VISUALIZE THE CONNECTION BETWEEN XYLOPHONE AND SOLFEGE LADDER

- Once the solfege ladder and the xylophone have been created, they may be saved as templates.
- The Xylophone may be rotated using the Green Rotate circle so that the bars can be aligned with the solfege ladder.
- The solfege ladder may be moved depending on which pitch is *do*.
- This reinforces the understanding between solfege pitch names and absolute pitch names. The former is movable while the latter is fixed.

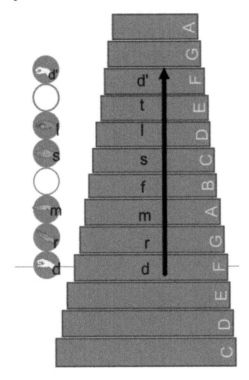

CREATE AN ANIMATED RECORDER

The animated recorder may be created using Basic Shapes – oval, rectangle, circle, triangle and the Object Animation – Fade In or Fade Out options.

For the Fade Out recorder, the covered holes need to be clicked to reveal open holes. For the Fade In recorder, the open holes need to be clicked or touched to be covered.

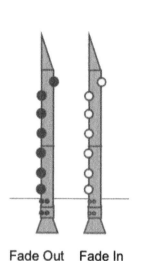

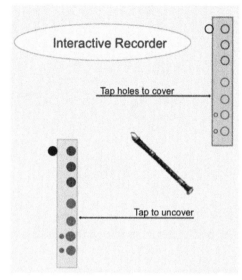

Fade Out   Fade In

- Select an oval from the Shapes menu, and draw one on the page.

- Clone this shape and place it above the previous one.

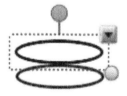

- Select both of these shapes, click on the drop down arrow to select Properties, and fill in the shapes.

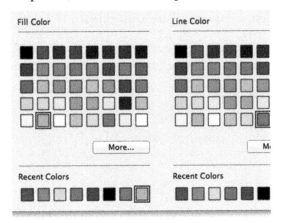

- From the Shapes menu, select Circle and draw one inside an oval. Draw a smaller circle beside it. Clone this and repeat for the second oval.

- Draw or clone 5 circles so they line up.

• Draw a rectangle around these circles.

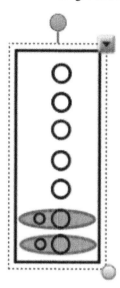

• Select the rectangle and select Order. Send to Back from the drop down menu. This will ensure that the rectangle is behind the circles and ovals.

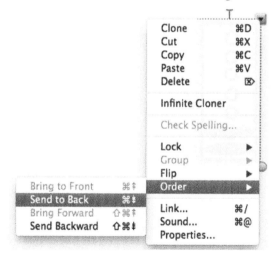

- Select the Line and Fill Color for the rectangle.

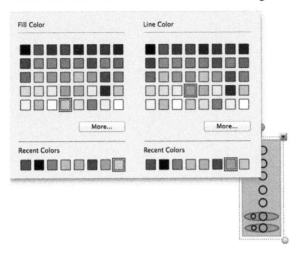

- Draw or clone one of the circles and position it to indicate the thumb/back hole for the recorder.
- This is now a basic template for fingering. Select all the objects, Group and Lock them in Place.

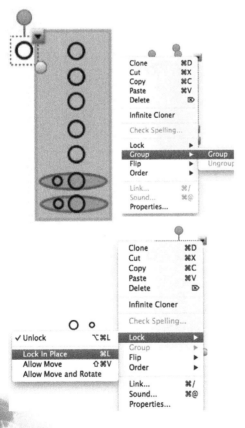

• Create identical circles as the ones used and Fill them in with black.

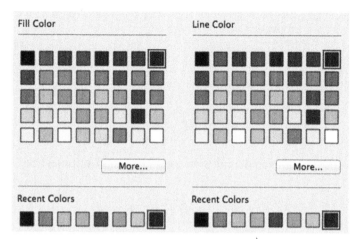

• Clone this and place the black circles over all the holes. Do the same for the little circles.

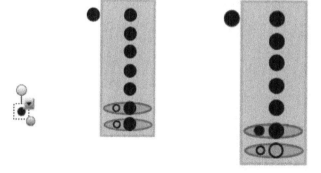

Fade In
• Select all the circles.
• Select Properties, and the Object Animation menu.

- Select the Fade In option when Object is clicked. This ensures that the black circles appear when the holes are tapped.

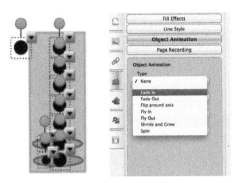

Fade Out

- For the holes to appear covered, and to be tapped to uncover, select the Fade Out option.

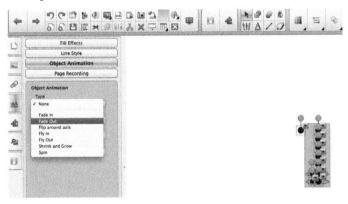

NOTE: The initial recorder will have open holes. The animation will appear when a hole is tapped or clicked.

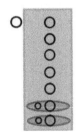

Fingering Activity

A simple activity is to draw a note and ask students to tap in the correct fingering, or for the teacher to tap in the fingering and to ask students to write the correct pitch on the staff.

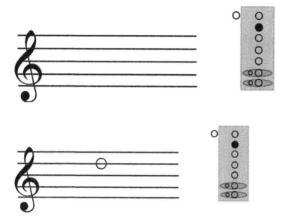

EXPORT IMAGES TO TABLETS

Pages in SMART Notebook, Charts in ActivInspire, Slides in Keynote and PowerPoint may be exported as image files. These files can be sent to digital tablets in the manner discussed in Chapter 2.
- Create the assessments or flashcards in one of the above applications.
- From the File menu, choose the Export As option.

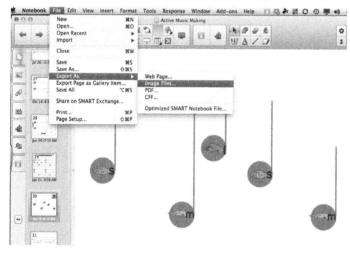

- Select Image Files

- Provide a name and a destination folder from which these may be retrieved as attachments in an email or uploads to Google Drive or Dropbox.

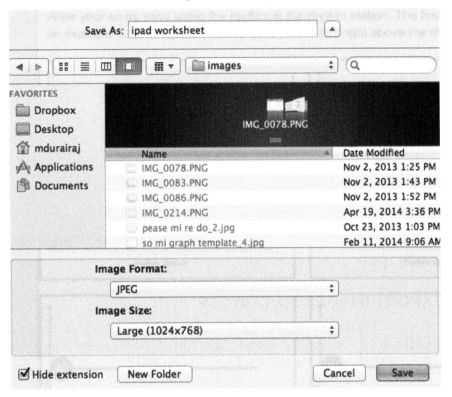

NOTE: Smart Notebook also has many flash and non-flash based widgets that can make presentations, assessments, and games interesting and engaging for all types of learners. The Lesson Activity Toolkit subfolder in the Gallery Essentials folder provides many sample activities for reference.

CONCLUSION

The ideas presented in this book are meant to be a starting point for inspiration. The activities presented are in themselves just one representation of the myriad possibilities. The basic features of various applications and apps presented here may be immediately applied to other activities, assessments and lessons. As one becomes more comfortable in creating and using the features, it is a simple transition to move to more sophisticated features like SMART response for computers and tablets, or to use apps like Plickers, Socrative, e-Clicker, Edmodo, and so many others for assessments and quizzes.

The possibilities of actively engaging in music making with technology are limitless!